African Tales

David P. Harvey

African Tales

David P. Harvey

Published by
PRAOTES PUBLISHING
1670 Salem Road
Cranbrook, BC, v1c 6v3
Canada
http://www.Praotes.Net

First Edition: October 2009

Copyright © 2009 David P. Harvey

ISBN: 1449572421

EAN-13: 9781449572426

Dedication

To my dear wife, Peggy,
who has demonstrated her devotion to her Lord
by humbly serving her Savior, her husband, her children,
and thousands of Africans to the glory of God.

Foreword

Dr. David Harvey blesses us with some poignant stories of his life during more than three decades of living in the forest country of Guinea, West Africa. From tales of snakes to malaria, fires to medicines: The miraculous hand of God is evident in the way He protected, provided, and proved Himself faithful in the lives of Dr. Harvey and his family.

I regard this autobiography of value for several reasons.

Our Lord Jesus declares in Revelation 12: 11 "And they overcame him by the blood of the Lamb, and by the word of their testimony." The word of their testimony. The most powerful of these words are - of course - the words of our own adventures with God. But the adventures and experiences of others help us remember that life with the Lord our God is dynamic, relational and highly personal. And that He is more than able to save.

Dr. Harvey also provides us with an anthropological perspective on the African country of Guinea. Further, his autobiography demonstrates how the Christian and Missionary Alliance approached the challenge of World Missions in the first decades following the Second World War.

African Tales reads very pleasantly. The chapters are short, making it an excellent book to read aloud with loved ones. Together experiencing Africa in the days when Blackberries were still berries and not yet hand-held multi-media devices.

Join Dr. Harvey and his family in their historic African Tales. And in the process rejoice, and praise the One who made it all possible.

Hans J.A. Dekkers
Publisher

Table of Contents

Introduction ---------------------------- 9

Picture Album -------------------------- 11

Wet Feet ------------------------------- 29

They Actually Sent Us! ----------------- 33

Music of Sorts ------------------------- 37

The Deep Forest ------------------------ 41

Nursing a la Africain ------------------ 45

Two Holes in the Floor ----------------- 49

Baptismal Happenings ------------------- 53

"One Lord, one faith, one baptism"...one cup! ---- 57

God Cares Even About Car Parts --------- 61

Two Beautiful Blessings ---------------- 67

"Please Forgive Me" -------------------- 71

A True Snake Story --------------------- 75

Lassa Fever ---------------------------- 79

Only God Could Do It! ------------------ 83

The Secret ----------------------------- 87

A Demonstration of God's Grace --------- 91

A Choice to Make ----------------------- 95

Mixed Emotions ------------------------- 99

An Unforgettable Bush Trip ------------ 101

Standing in the Plate ----------------- 105

Au revoir ----------------------------- 107

Introduction

Many folks have lived in Africa who were not from that culture. As missionaries who arrived in West Africa in 1957, my wife and I experienced numerous incidents known only to us and a few of our colleagues, many of whom have already passed to their heavenly rewards. Also, many of the happenings which transpired in our early days in Guinea, West Africa, may be known only to us.

Why should I write about them now? Why should *you* know about them? For one thing, I want to leave some kind of record for my children and grandchildren. For another, God taught us lessons that just might benefit others. Looking back over the past 50 years or so, I stand amazed at God's protection, His faithfulness, His mercy and grace, and the abounding love which He manifested to us, His simple, and often erring children.

For over three decades, my family and I experienced what can only be termed "miraculous events" when we look back and see how ignorant we were of the culture in which we lived and of the Kissi people whom we loved. We had been sent by The Christian and Missionary Alliance.

For the record, my wife, Peggy, was born in Africa. Her parents, Michael and Helen Kurlak, had been some of the earliest missionaries to Guinea and worked among the Maninka tribe for years. Peggy's parents were unable to return to the country because of President Sekou Toure's edict. Being a missionary kid is quite different than being an adult missionary, even if you return as an adult to the same land. Furthermore, my wife, Peggy, had been assigned with me to a different region of the country, a different tribal group from where she had grown up.

At the time we were missionaries in Guinea (1957-1987), the country went from being a colony of the French to become one of the first independent countries in that part of the world. The first president of the country, Sekou Toure, was an avowed

Marxist and he left an indelible impression on the land which, until this day, bears the scars of his regime. Only God knows the extent of the horrors which so many faced in the prisons of the capital city or in other areas of the country where people were forced to do what the Party required them to do.

Through all of that time the Church grew and prospered in that land, and no matter the circumstances that surrounded His people, they stood strong and courageous and were testimonies of God's grace and power. We were privileged to live among a tribe from which many responded to God's salvation message. And it is among these Kissi people that we experienced so many of God's marvelous acts. I want you to know some of what we encountered. It is a witness to God's mighty love and faithfulness.

David P. Harvey September 2009

African Tales

David and Peggy sail for Africa 1956.

Four babies Peggy had delivered.

African Tales

Village chief's huts on fire (Chapter 1: Wet Feet).

David and Peggy, with Peggy's parents (circa 1957).

Our two children, Judy and Jim.

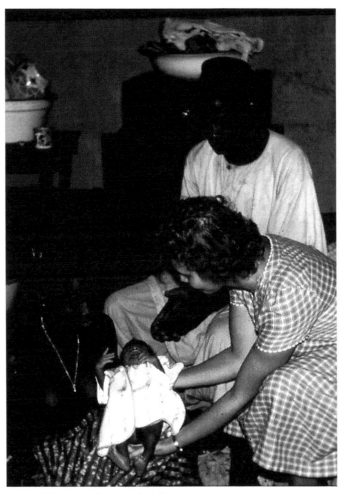
Peggy delivers baby in a dark hut.

Traveling in Africa has its own problems.

Map of Guinea.

African Tales

Witch doctor with Balaphone (Chapter 3: Music of Sorts).

Kids always crowd around.

Our first home in Guinea.

Kissi-region pastors with whom David worked.

Walking in the deep forest (Chapter 4: The Deep Forest).

Peggy visits with Guinean woman.

Rainy season presented problems of its own.

David and his python (Chapter 12: A True Snake Story).

Chapter 1

Wet Feet

The black smoke billowed up in the sky as the cries and screams of the crowd reached us on our back porch. We had been treating ill patients that morning as usual when the commotion caused us to change course. Why all the frenzy across the market place from our humble dwelling? This was the year 1958 and a lot of political shenanigans were taking place in Guinea.

I ran to the edge of road and began to ask questions of anyone who would be patient enough to understand my version of French. I was told that the village chief was holed up in one of his huts while another hut was burning—one in which he had his rice stored. I dared to get closer to the commotion and found that many men had machetes in their hands and were threatening the life of the chief and other of his relatives who were holding home-made shotguns.

It was obvious, at least to me, that a lot of bloodshed was on the horizon unless something was done before sundown. Racing back to the house, I told my wife to halt the dispensing of medicines; that it was urgent that we take off for Kissidougou, the main town in that part of the forest region.

The village in which this tragedy seemed about to happen was Yende-Millimou. This was a "market village" of over 1,000 people, made up of folks from a number of different tribes. Most of the village folk were either Kissi or Maninka, but there was a sprinkling of Fulas and other tribal folk who made this rather large village their home.

Our mud-brick home was located just across from the market place. It had housed the village caravansary, the local "motel" for people passing through, before our arrival in that town. A missionary colleague, Ralph Shellrude, had persuaded the town folk to rent it to the mission for at least a couple of years and that became our home. It was now a three-room house which my wife had fixed up so that to me, at least, it seemed like an oasis in that not-too-clean village. That home also became the area clinic where all sorts of sick folk and pregnant women found a caring hand and a loving heart to minister to their needs.

On this day, however, all the caring came to an abrupt end. We got into our 1954 Dodge truck and headed for the large center of Kissidougou. In that town was found the French Governor of that region and I knew he had French military personnel who kept some semblance of order in the territory under his command. We were on our way to see him.

As we reached the edge of the village, we found that there was already a blockade across the road. Men with large sticks and machetes were standing in the middle of the road. "Where are you going?" one of the men shouted as for a moment a sickening sense of fear gripped me. I tried to look as if this was a normal trip I would be taking to Kissidougou so I simply told the man where I was headed. "We know you have friends up there," he replied "so make your visit and don't see anyone else." "I'll be back as soon as I can," I replied. "I am not taking anybody with me from the village." This seemed to satisfy him and he let me go. I was actually shaking, but held on to the steering wheel to try and minimize the showing of any unusual emotion.

As we drove the next 25 miles on a winding, dirt road to Kissidougou, we thanked the Lord that we had passed the first hurdle and were on our way to see if we could get some French military men to come to Yende (short for Yende-Millimou) to prevent what could be . . . many people hacked to death in a senseless slaughter.

The French Governor greeted me warmly and I relayed to him the urgency of the moment. "If it were at all possible," I pleaded, "could you send some troops to Yende to quell a riot that is going on there now?" He immediately called in his commander and the troops were on their way within the hour. "You had better stay here in Kissidougou for a couple of days," he warned me, and I agreed that his counsel was probably very wise.

For two days my wife and I stayed in the home of Earl and Peggy Stewart, missionary teachers at the Telekoro Bible Institute. We relaxed and prayed and wondered: What had gone on down in Yende during our absence? It wasn't long before we would find out.

After our two days of rest and prayer, we got into our Dodge truck and began the trip back along the dusty, twisty road to Yende. Even though we had prayed, we found that some fear and apprehension still gripped us as we crossed that last wooden bridge and made our way into our "hometown." What would we find? Had anyone tried to enter and ransack our dwelling? How would we be treated by the villagers who had known we had left town and subsequently asked the French to send troops to their village?

It didn't take long to find out. Shortly after our truck pulled into the yard and we got out of our vehicle, people came running over to us and began to thank us profusely for helping to avoid a disaster in their town. "O, Monsieur, merci, merci, merci," they shouted over and over. "So many people could have been killed; so much blood would have been shed,'" they yelled. "May God be praised!" someone else blurted out.

Whew! What a relief! And we *did* praise our God. He again proved faithful, calmed our fears, gave us favor with the people, and it appeared that our ministry there was now even more acceptable and welcomed among the villagers. The Lord had given us a special opening among a people with whom we would be working for the next eight years. Getting our feet wet that first year in Guinea proved to be an experience that helped shape our lives for the next thirty years.

Chapter 2
They Actually Sent Us!

The fact that we were in West Africa was a story in itself. Talk about green timber! My wife, Peggy, and I were greener than green and yet the people in the Foreign Department of The Christian and Missionary Alliance (C&MA) had actually told us they were sending us overseas. Peggy was still only 21 years of age and I was a ripe old 23! Let me tell you about God's calling and grace towards two young people whom God sent to the other side of the world.

I had recently graduated from John Brown University (JBU) and Peggy had just become a registered nurse. Peggy and I got married and attended St. Paul Bible College in St. Paul, Minnesota. We also applied for missionary service knowing that God had called us. So we were willing to serve Him wherever He might direct us. Both of us thought it would probably be in Indonesia as that was our first choice on the missionary application form.

St. Paul Bible College (now Crown College) was offering an advanced bachelor's degree. If one had a bachelor's degree from an accredited college, one could then receive a Th.B degree in missions. In that same class with me were men destined to become well-known servants of God: Bob Henry, Joe Tewinkle, David Volstad and others. The professors of missions in that program were Dr. Jack Shepherd and Dr. Lynwood Barney.

Peggy also enrolled as a full-time student and both of us worked at what was then known as Miller Hospital. I was a lowly orderly and my wife had the opportunity ---and took it— of being able to tell me what to do! We've had a good many laughs over some of the incidents that took place in that work environment.

In 1955 the Foreign Department of the C&MA had desired to send out 102 missionaries in the coming year. During the year of 1956 they were seeking to fill that quota. Couples like the Paul Alfords and Edward Maxeys were sent out that same year. I am not certain, but it appears we may have been the last two of that 102. We were deployed in August of that year and sailed for France on a small Italian ship to begin French language study in Paris.

God must have had His hand in that appointment. In January of 1955 I had graduated from JBU and went directly to St. Paul. The Foreign Department must have credited my time as "preaching-point minister" at JBU as sufficient ministry experience. During my last two years of college I had a regular preaching post in one of the rural Arkansas communities.

What tipped the balance, I am sure, was the fact that my wife had been born in West Africa, grew up speaking the trade language (Maninka) and was quite fluent in French. Her parents were C&MA missionaries and my parents were in the ministry with the C&MA. That probably didn't hurt either! We were so young and rather immature. God was going to have to use some pretty raw material!

There are certain advantages, however, to being young. The learning of a new language as well as the understanding of a different culture in a new country is usually easier for the young. God knows we wanted to go! And in His mercy, He surrounded us with other more mature missionary couples like Ray and Lucille Stombaugh. During our time in France God had so much to teach us!

We lived with a French family on the fifth floor of a French apartment house and got our daily exercise by climbing stairs. We set out to study not only the French language, but also study and memorize the Scriptures. The first book we memorized together was the Epistle to the Philippians which we still know by heart today!

I eventually learned enough French to pass the language exams (Peggy didn't have much trouble doing that!) and we then boarded another ship for passage to West Africa. What a burst of mixed emotions (especially for me!) as we stepped ashore and were met by Peggy's parents! If had known what actually lay ahead of us at that point, I might not have been so light-hearted. But we knew we were where God wanted us to be. God had certainly opened many doors for us and we were so glad to walk through them!

Chapter 3
Music of Sorts

I play the marimba. From my earliest memory of playing a toy xylophone as a small child, I loved to bang out any tune I could remember. Hardly an accomplished musician, I *can* play a marimba with four mallets and sound like I know what I am doing! It is a rather deceptive skill since I can barely read music and I play the marimba mostly by ear. I can play almost any tune I know if I can choose my own key in which to play! I still play in my local church and have played in quite a few churches around the country including towns like St. Louis, Chicago, Fort Myers, and of course Toccoa, Georgia! And I have even played in Yende-Millimou! The marimba has been such a significant part of my life that I just had to take it to Africa with me.

Therein lies some interesting facets of my musical career. The marimba is a large instrument, not easily moved from place to place. Nevertheless, I took it to Africa for my own enjoyment, hoping as well that I might be able to use it in some kind of ministry there. Occasionally, I did play at some C&MA field conferences (now called *field forums or field retreats*) in the town of Kankan where our conferences were annually held in what some might call "those early years." But that was limited to three conferences as I remember.

My desire was to use the marimba for ministry among the Kissi people where God had placed us. It wasn't long before I began to take my marimba on evangelistic ministries out into the villages that surrounded our own town of Yende. As I look back upon those many ventures, I can only smile and wonder what I was thinking!

It would take three of us to get the marimba into the back of the pickup. Two fellows would then stay in the back of the truck (although there were usually at least ten people in there!) holding on to the instrument as we drove slowly to the village we had chosen to evangelize. The village might lie along the main dirt road (filled with potholes) or it may have been a village off the road where we often followed a foot path with the pickup batting down the tall elephant grass as we inched along.

Upon arrival, we would then carry the instrument—it is fairly heavy—to the place the village chief or elder designated as the location for our evening service. These evangelistic services were always held following the evening meal which would be after the people had returned from their fields. No services would be held, of course, unless permission had been granted by the village chief and/or medicine man. At times there would be opposition to our holding a service but, for the most part, permissions were freely granted.

After a hymn or two sung by the Kissi Christians who had ridden with us in the truck, I would step up and play the marimba. Even now I laugh as I think of it. I did not see *them* laugh, but I do not know why they would not have. Here I was, playing a hymn on the marimba-- a tune they probably never heard of—and playing in close harmony, which happens to be my style of playing because it is what I hear.

It is not, however, what they hear! It must have been just plain weird for these folks, Christians and pagans alike, to hear such strange sounds belted out by a white man playing an oversized *balaphone* (native xylophone). Songs they didn't know, played (at least to them) in a discordant manner. Come to think of it, they never seemed too thrilled by my music. Never any clapping but always polite enough to not ask me what on earth I thought I was doing!

This Americanized *balaphone* did serve as an interesting drawing card for children, however. So for almost eight years I repeated this event. Near the end of our fourth term I realized that my talents at playing the marimba would be best left Stateside, so I shipped my marimba home and kept it someone's basement for almost 20 years!

Before I packed up the marimba to send it to the States, however, it was involved in an incident which I will never forget. One day, out on the road in front of our house, a medicine man, with painted face and colorful feathers in his hair, passed by. He was playing a *balaphone* as he led a group of young lads who had just come from their circumcision in the bush. He stopped by our driveway and kept on playing his *balaphone*.

Foolishly, I went out to talk to him and told him I played one of those too. "I would like to see it," he offered. So I invited him into my house to see the marimba which took up a good part of our living room. He picked up the mallets which were lying on the wooden keys, and started to bang on my marimba. I could feel satanic power as he wailed away on the keys. Our cat screeched and scooted under the small couch nearby.

Quickly, I pulled the sheet over the marimba and ushered the man and his companions out of the house. It was the scariest thing I had ever encountered to that point. I learned a lesson the hard way. How foolish it was to invite a witchdoctor into my home, not with the intention of witnessing to him, but simply to show off a musical instrument. That incident left me shaking in my shoes as, in a real sense, I felt the power of the Enemy and heard music which I hoped never to hear again.

Chapter 4

The Deep Forest

Allegedly, our home village of Yende-Millimou was in the forest country. Due to the slash-and-burn way of life, however, the forests had been much depleted in our area. Further south, in the southwestern territory of the Kissi tribe, the deep forests of the region were still in abundance.

My wife and I were initiated by Ralph Shellrude on our first evangelistic trip into these forests on a two-week foray into these dark, wooded areas. As we left the Land Rover in a village on the side of a dirt road, we picked up some carriers who were willing, for a price, to carry the necessary items we thought needed for life in the forest.

Included in the loads were aluminum cots, sheets and towels, mosquito nets, a lantern, folding chairs, filtered water, a small kerosene stove, and some food items. We thought it necessary to carry in some French bread, peanut butter, jam, and a few canned goods such as baked beans and spaghetti. We had no idea what we would find deep in the dark forest.

What a sight we were as we walked single file on the winding path through the tall elephant grass. Under the hot African sun, we would stop every half hour or so to take some sips of water. My wife and I hadn't, as yet, learned the Kissi language so we didn't speak much as we walked for what seemed to be eternity. The tall grass swished against our bare arms as we tried to keep up with these Kissi men moving rapidly towards the village of Ndema.

The forest was getting thicker as we progressed towards the village. Very large trees, some looking hundreds of years old, were everywhere. Near the village, we had seen some rice cakes and other items at the base of some of these large trees. This was a sign to us that these were trees before which sacrifices had been made to the spirits of their ancestors.

Villagers had been awaiting our arrival. No caucasians had ever been in this area before so we were somewhat of a sideshow, I suspect, to these people as we arrived with all we thought necessary to survive. We were welcomed by the village chief and shown two huts in which we were to be lodged during our stay. I was so glad that we were in grass-roofed huts. Houses with tin roofs proved to be very hot during the day, especially if they had no ceilings. While we found some pan-roofed houses to be somewhat cleaner than grass-roofed ones because there was no falling debris and few lizards, it seemed that entering a grass-roofed hut was like coming into an air-conditioned room!

We were soon welcomed in the traditional way with many "How-are-yous?," "How is your wife?," "How are your children?," "How are your chickens?," and all the "How are" questions! Then we were given some bananas, some kola nuts and, to top it all off, a small goat which we presented back to them so that they could cook it for our supper.

Peggy and I set up our cots and our mosquito nets, placing other items on a wooden table while trying to ignore the strong manure smell of a floor freshly layered to show how welcome we were. Ralph had taught us how to find some branches and to tie up the nets. We were ready to just flop down on the cots and get some needed rest before the evening meal and the service which was to follow.

It appeared to us that the whole village turned out to hear us (probably to just gawk at us!). After singing a few choruses in the Kissi language, Peggy and I gave our testimonies in English (translated by Ralph), and then he gave a simple message of how God's love had provided a Savior for sin. I learned later that he had to explain sin at length to let them know what it was in God's eyes and what God's book had to say about it.

What a joy to see many indicate they wanted to believe in this One God had sent for them. So we stayed a few days while Ralph taught them—and we helped where we could—so we could leave them with at least some knowledge of what living for Christ entailed.

I cannot express on paper what joy filled my heart during those days in that village hidden in the deep forest of southern Guinea. It was as if I was doing just what God created me for; as if all that I had prepared for had come to fruition there in that one village. I was actually telling people about Jesus in a place where, if we had not gone, they would have had no other opportunity to hear.

No one in the outside world knew these people existed. Who cared? How would they ever hear if we didn't tell them? God had permitted us, along with Ralph, to be his messengers, to these people in the dark forests of Guinea. I believe that one day on Heaven's shores, we will be singing praises to the Lamb alongside some of these forest people. "Amazing love, how can it be, that thou my God, should die for me (and them)?" What amazing grace! What an awesome privilege was ours! It is truly indescribable.

Chapter 5
Nursing a la Africain

"I never dreamed I would be doing that!" Those words have come from the lips or to the mind of most missionaries and for my wife, a registered nurse, they would come often. Having worked in a hospital for one year prior to going to the field, Peggy found herself involved in some things a nurse might do at home, but also ministering in ways she had never even dreamed of!

One could say that almost all missionaries have been involved in diagnosing, as well as treating, different kinds of illnesses and patients for which they have had no training. Peggy found that opening a dispensary in Yende would result in challenges which called for more than human reason and training. God *did* give her wisdom beyond her years and experience. This resulted in people and villages opening up to the gospel story.

Many of the folk who came to our clinic had heard from their neighbors or friends that a white woman had brought healing medicines that were given without cost. The government had recognized our dispensary and, every other month, offered a limited amount of medicines and medical supplies which were of great benefit to the villagers. These medicines included antibiotics for yaws, malaria treatments, anti-venom for snake bites, and other useful medicinal supplies.

We, of course, had brought some items with us and we were also able to obtain help from the dispensary at the Telekoro Bible Institute. It seemed that we readily used up everything that came our way. From morning till evening folks would come line up outside our door. Villagers would arrive with large, open sores, babies burning up with fever, children with all kinds of needs which no one could help us diagnose.

Then there were the pregnant women. Ladies would show up at all hours of the day and night and ask for help so that their relative's baby could be delivered safely. What complications ensued! At times it would be a hydrocephalic little one. Sometimes the mother would be very sick at the time of delivery. Often there were twins. At times, I was even called in "to help push." More often than not, especially in the middle of the night, I would lie in bed and pray as Peggy was in some hut in the middle of the village doing all she could to assure a safe delivery.

People would often bring their small children who were at death's door. Their child, who may have been sick for weeks, was probably at the mercy of the witchdoctor for a long time. When the family realized the child was not going to make it, they would bring the young one to us, hoping against hope that our medicine would prove stronger than theirs. Often, it was not helpful. And it could, at times, present quite a predicament. If you gave a shot and the baby died, they could accuse you of killing the baby. If you did nothing, you would be seen, of course, as having no mercy. Peggy always did something—and of course prayed--trusting that God would touch the little one for His own glory.

So often the unexpected happened; a dramatic turn-around would occur. God, in His mercy, would put His divine touch on the little one and raise him/her up. Or the one who had been bitten by a snake (we didn't even see) would survive. The news would spread and villages would open up to the gospel. People would listen to the Word preached. Some would repent and believe and be added to the Church.

Peggy would do everything from pulling rotten teeth to sewing up the buttocks of one who had fallen from a palm tree! We would at times end up walking miles and miles to a small village on a hill shrouded by huge mango trees, hoping to save a life with an injection of anti-malarial vaccine. Sometimes, after hours of walking, we would arrive at the village, only to find that we were too late. We could only give our condolences, offer a prayer, and trust that the love shown would redound to God's glory.

There were some wonderful, joyous moments. I recall when the pastor's wife of the Kissidougou church was taken to the hospital as her twins were due to be born. The family wanted us to help, as they knew that the only doctor assigned to the hospital was a man from Eastern Europe who despised the people he was sent to help.

We entered the hospital room to find the pastor's wife lying naked on the table, her stomach extended as the twins were not too far from term. A C-section was about to be performed. As the surgeon was using the scalpel, cutting open the womb to extract the babies, an old African woman was sweeping the floor! The pastor's wife was crying out in pain and the doctor was yelling at her for being so noisy! The dust circulating in the room was visible by the light of the naked bulb hanging in that dingy operating room. Additionally, the doctor told us that the hospital was out of antibiotics.

But in spite of everything, two beautiful baby boys were born! Peggy was holding one upside down, while another nurse—an African assistant--was taking care of the other one. I was praying and rejoicing in what I had beheld. God had overruled in a very difficult and awkward situation (that we were even allowed to participate was a miracle!) and healthy twins were born. Peggy administered some antibiotics from the Bible school dispensary when the mother was taken to another room. I have only partially described what took place. You could not believe what we actually saw! But God in His mercy and grace brought triumph out of tragedy. And the pastor's wife came through with a strong testimony of God's help and deliverance.

Chapter 6
Two Holes in the Floor

Many of the villages in which we preached the gospel were some distance from our own village of Yende. Kassadou was one town where the good news had never been proclaimed. One day a messenger from that village came to let us know they too wanted to hear the "Jesus story." We were more than happy to oblige.

The local pastor and some singers accompanied me. Off we drove in our 4-wheel drive pick-up to this village many kilometers away in the bush. We traveled over very rough terrain which only a four-wheel drive vehicle could navigate. And we did it slowly. Thus it was fairly late when we finally came upon this village tucked away in the dense Kissi forest.

After the proper greetings and permission were given, we were shown the huts in which we would sleep after the service. I had not brought my wife on this particular trip as there were a number of sick people who urgently needed her attention at home. So I had a hut to myself. Since the villagers knew we were coming, they had already prepared the hut by laying fresh cow manure on the floor. That was akin to vacuuming the rugs before strangers arrive. The odor let one know it had been done fairly recently!

After I sat in the hut for a few minutes, folks arrived to present their gifts of bananas and cola nuts. Then the pastor arrived in my hut with some other village folks to present us all with a rooster as the final gift. I had learned by this time that the proper response was not only a "thank you for the gift" but also the words "show it the knife." This indicated that you were giving the chicken back to them so that they could kill it and prepare it for the evening meal to follow.

After the delicious chicken and rice meal, the cow horn was blown calling the villagers to the service. On this particular occasion, it appeared that the whole village was gathered to hear the message we would proclaim. At the conclusion of the message, a number of people responded that they wanted to follow the Jesus way.

By this time in our missionary career, we had realized that often these "first responders" didn't have a very good grasp of the gospel message. For the most part, many were signaling their initial interest in the gospel and were saying by their response, "Yes, we hear and believe and what we understand so far we accept as true." Only God knows when new birth actually occurs. For some it may be at the moment we see them respond to the invitation. For others, it may be way down the road. At this particular moment, I found myself in a hut with some of those who had responded, going over the gospel story and seeking to guide these inquirers into what I was praying would be saving faith. Only God knew what was transpiring in the hearts of these seekers.

It was now after 11:00 p.m. Exhausted from the long trip, all the necessary greetings, and dealing with people after the message of the evening, I was sound asleep on my cot in the cool hut.

A knock came on the door. "Who is it?" I wearily asked. "It is I" came the familiar reply. "Who are you?" I queried. "I was one who believed tonight. I want you to come and see my house." Was I hearing correctly? Did I hear a man asking me to come and see his house in the middle of the night? No, it wasn't a dream. A man was actually standing outside my door asking me to go and see his dwelling.

I pulled on my trousers and slipped out the door. Before I knew it I was walking past goats and sheep in the village and following this man up a hill on which his newly-built house was situated. There I found the Christians who had traveled with me from Yende, plus a number of other folk who had joined them on top of the hill.

Kekoura's house was not like the others in the village. He had an aluminum roof and newly poured concrete floors. It turns out he had been in the military and had fought for the French in Vietnam. With his extra money he had built a house quite superior to the average hut owned by the typical villager.

"Come inside," he said. "When I built this house I asked the witch doctor what I needed to do to protect this dwelling and my family. He told me to pay him so much money and he gave me a fetish to bury in the floor here." With that he grabbed a pickax and began to dig a hole in the floor against the protests of many of the others gathered there.

He knew right where the fetish was located. After breaking up the cement and then digging further into the dirt, he came up with a liter bottle of liquid. It was brownish in color and looked like it may have had some blood mixed in it. "Follow me," he blurted out. So we followed Kekoura to the far edge of the hill where he threw the bottle forcefully down into a ravine.

"I don't need that anymore," he called out. "Now that I believe in Jesus, He is the One who will protect me from now on!" What was I hearing? Could it be true that this man, who had just heard and believed the gospel this very evening, was giving evidence of his faith and demonstrating to everyone that his trust was in his newly found Lord? "Come back to the house," he yelled out to us all. "I am not finished yet." He then told us that he never really did trust that witch doctor, and so to be sure of his home's protection, he had visited a Muslim imam who had given him a leather amulet (for a price) to wear around his neck for a time and then bury under his bedroom floor.

So here he was again with the pickax. Down it came until he had broken up the cement floor in his bedroom. He had not forgotten where he had buried this amulet. After digging in the dirt for a time, up he came with a package wrapped in banana leaves, now turned a gooey black color.

He took out the amulet to show us and then walked over to the ravine. 'Don't throw that away," I told him. "I would like to take it to show my people what you had put your trust in." "No," he replied. "I don't want this old thing around anymore" and he quickly threw it over the ravine.

Back to his house he went with all of us following behind him. As we approached the house, some of his friends began to put the dirt back into the holes in the floor and even tried to put back some of the broken pieces of cement. "Don't do that!" he yelled. I thought the man was beside himself.

He bent over and took the dirt out of the holes and threw the pieces of cement out the door. "Listen," he said. "A lot of people come to see me and my new house. Now when they come they will surely ask, "Kekoura, why do you have two holes in your floor?" "And I'll tell them about Jesus. I will tell them that He is all you need. I will tell them that He is the Savior, the protector, the provider of all."

I was speechless. Here was a man who had heard the gospel for the first time, repented of his sins and believed in Jesus Christ just a few hours ago, and now was demonstrating a faith and trust in His Lord which, to me, was astounding. God had wrought a miracle (actually, more than one), and this man bore witness to the power of God and to what a changed life could truly be.

More than three decades later at a *Jesus 2000 Rally* held in Conkary, the capital, I met a man at the close of a meeting at which I had spoken. "Do you remember, Kekoura?" he asked. "I certainly do," I replied. "I am his son," the man said, "and he is still following the Jesus way, as am I." I grasped his hand heartily and began to recount to him (although he already knew!) my recollection of the miracle of God's grace in his father's heart. He told me the two holes were still in the floor of his father's house. I still get goose bumps today when I think of what those two holes represent.

Chapter 7
Baptismal Happenings

Baptism and Africa. That phrase conjures up a lot in one's mind, especially if the hearers of those words had worked with the Christian Church in Africa. Baptism is extremely important. You do not have to believe in baptismal regeneration to know that baptism is linked to salvation in the Scriptures. All you have to do is read passages relating to Pentecost, Philip and the Ethiopian, or Paul, Silas and the Philippian jailer (plus many other passages) to understand that truth.

I am fairly sure however, that less than half of those who claim to be Christian in Africa have been baptized. Perhaps that is true world-wide. I know, however, that there are numerous reasons given for the lack of Christians being baptized on the Dark Continent.

People will cite polygamy, the lack of clergy (or ordained clergy), the lack of teaching on baptism, the fear of reprisal or any number of reasons why there are so many un-baptized believers. Certainly, there are mission and church policies in place where blame can be placed. And hopefully more will be done to see that this command of our Lord's is carried out in the months and years ahead.

Most of the people this writer has baptized have been in West Africa. I have baptized them in flowing streams and stagnant ponds. I have immersed them in church baptisteries and in cool lakes. On one occasion there were so many believers being baptized at one time in a baptistery in the Ivory Coast that the water turned brown!

How could I ever forget the first African that I baptized? It happened in the Guekedou Region of Guinea in the village of Nongoa. A young lady, previously demonized, had come to Christ and wanted to be baptized immediately. I was so glad to oblige her. We found a slow-moving stream at the edge of the village and with the believers singing joyfully to the beat of the tom-toms, we descended into the water.

Finda –she later took the name of Rachel--stepped into the water and gave a vibrant testimony of God's grace in bringing her salvation. As I bent over to put her under the water, my foot slipped on a slimy rock and I was re-baptized along with her!

People on the shore tried to keep from laughing and the singing helped cover my obvious embarrassment. But I know the color of my face changed to a bright shade of red even while the joy of what I had experienced reverberated in my heart. That young lady eventually came to Bible school and became the wife of one of our Kissi pastors.

Baptism in Africa carries other memories for me which are not ones easily forgotten. It seemed, to me at least, that almost every baptism in which I participated in a village setting was always "on the other side of the river." Why that was I may never know, but I do know that it was cause for many moments of embarrassing emotion.

Crossing most of these rivers meant that one had to traverse the trunk of a single palm tree which had been laid down to connect the two edges of the stream. At times the water below seemed to be very far down from the "bridge." It may have been a long way to the water, it may not have been. But it was always too far down for me!

I am not good when it comes to heights, and traversing a single (or double) palm-tree trunk was as difficult a task as one could ask of this missionary. The African women would walk briskly across the "bridge" with a baby on the back, one in her arms and even a load of wood on her head. I, however, would approach the trunk of that palm tree with fear and trepidation.

Placing my feet carefully on the tree trunk, I would start across, then hesitate. As I began to panic and shake, I would then gently sit down on the log and begin to scoot across on my back side. My wife, who would have already crossed, would be urging me on with a smile on her face. Of course I was the last one to cross over. Hopefully the other people on the other side kept going so as not to behold this frightened white man inching his way across the long palm log.

Baptisms were usually held in the dry season, with most of them on Christmas day or around that holiday time. As this was the time when the rivers were fairly low, it was much easier to find a suitable place for people to gather, where the water would be at a proper depth. Last but not least, the crocodiles were usually looking for fuller streams of water at this time of the year.

Oh, the joy of seeing followers of Christ obey Him in baptism! Despite the embarrassing times, despite the fact that there were elements surrounding those events which may have brought some hesitation, no experience in life could be so moving and so exhilarating as to see one who has come to faith in Christ follow Him in this act of obedience. Even as I write these words, my mind and heart are filled with thanksgiving for having been a part of so many of these marvelous times of worship, praise, and boundless joy.

Chapter 8
"One Lord, one faith, one baptism"
...one cup!

They never prepared us for this in any mission class in which I had participated. But here I was, leading the communion service in our village, and there was only one cup. It should not have even mattered, I suppose, but being a first-term missionary, and facing the situation for the first time, I found myself thinking other thoughts than those of what this event should signify to us gathered there to celebrate the Lord's Supper.

Perhaps there were about eighty of us gathered there that Sunday morning. I could see that some of those were older folk. Others I knew had experienced a degree of leprosy in the past. There were the folk coughing in the crowd of congregants. And there were those with diseases known only to the Creator.

This experience was one which would lead this writer to request of friends at home to try and send a set of individual plastic communion cups which I knew were used in communions services in the States. But we were not as yet at that juncture. Furthermore, since I was leading this communion service, it was I who would be the last to drink of this single cup after it had made the rounds.

It may have been easier had we been serving real wine. But the grape Kool-Aid which we were using would certainly be no guarantee that any germs would be erased at any point in the consumption of the liquid. My wife had put it all together and at least we had used filtered water! As I thanked the Lord for what this cup represented to us all, I also breathed a silent prayer for protection for my own health.

I am sure it was an unnecessary prayer. Certainly the Lord would watch over His servants as they celebrated His death and coming again, but we are only human. At times our faith is weak. At times we do not reason correctly. We revert to fleshly thinking, not spiritual, and this should not be. But I am trying in this writing to be honest, and let you know the reality of what really happened. Also, I want you to try and understand what was going through my mind when I should have been dwelling on more spiritual matters.

The Church had a ruling, in Guinea at least, that only ordained clergy could serve communion. Since there were only two of us at that time in the whole Kissi district who had passed ordination, I was often called upon to serve communion in the remotest places. The Christians were desperate to obey their Lord in observing His Table, and there were few of us who could meet that need.

We had little to work with in terms of the elements for celebrating the Lord's Table. "Bread" included many different kinds of food such as banana chips, rice cakes, sweet potato fries, and even stale popcorn that I had brought along. Actual bread was not always readily available. Sometimes we had been away from home for two weeks or more so anything like bread we may have brought with us, was not worth eating at the time of serving communion.

The "wine" was even more imaginative. We tried to have some kind of grape Kool-Aid available but we soon depleted that option. At times we used grape, strawberry, or any kind of colored jam mixed with water. You may remember something called Fizzies. This is a carbonated beverage that came in a small tablet which fizzed up when put with water. We took these with us (while they lasted) and they were something that could be substituted—if a very poor substitute—for grape juice.

At a large church conference held at Kankan one year, the Guinea pastors discovered very late that they had nothing for serving "the cup" at communion. It was already Sunday morning and they had no idea what they could use. They came to me and frantically asked if I could come up with something. The only beverage I possessed was two cans of Coca-Cola. So, mixing it with water, we actually served hundreds of believers. It wasn't tasty, and it didn't look like much when diluted, but it wasn't plain water. I am sure that the Lord smiled down upon His people gathered there as they remembered what Calvary meant.

Precious times around His Table in West Africa have been seared upon this memory. Seeing former fetish worshippers taking the sacred elements (whatever they might have been) under palm leaf shelters brings joy to this heart that only those who have experienced such a gift could ever imagine.

Chapter 9
God Cares Even About Car Parts

The Doug Millers were entering Guinea by road, through Liberia. I was to meet them at the border and bring them to their station at N'Zerekore. A cable had been sent by our US headquarters' personnel to Conakry and they had sent a "runner" to our town of Yende asking if I would meet the Millers at that forest town.

It was rainy season in Guinea and the road between Yende and N'Zerekore was, at places, quite treacherous and almost impassable. I had a four-wheel drive Jeep which seated five people with a little room in the back for extra baggage. I said goodbye to my wife whom I left to take care of the dispensary. I took along with me, instead, the boy who had been helping us with the house. His name was Paul. I knew that anything could happen on a trip such as this. And it did.

To reach N'Zerekore, one must drive to Guekedou, through the Kissi region and into the Toma tribal area. After crossing the river on a hazardous ferry, one would then reach the Guerze tribal territory, a region where the town of N'Zerekore was located. It would probably take a good part of a day so we left early in the morning.

As we left the Kissi tribal area and entered the region where the Toma people lived, I descended a rather high hill which was quite muddy. As I began to slip and slide, I decided to put the Jeep into four-wheel drive. Then I thought it best to put the vehicle in low-range so as to descend the hill very gradually and carefully.

As I put my foot on the clutch, the pedal went directly to the floorboard and the gearshift moved back and forth without resistance. Something wasn't working and I, for one, didn't know what had happened. We started to pick up speed, and when I cautiously braked, the car spun around and began careening down the hill. Bouncing off a tree which was just on the edge of a curve in the road, we finally found ourselves at the bottom of the hill, shaken up, but safe.

Paul said to me, "Mister, why don't we pray?" "Yes," I shot back, "I was going to do that." Of course I was. But probably not when he wanted me to! Actually, there was nothing else to do. We were in trouble in a strange area, and it was beginning to rain. Only God *could* help us now. And the Millers would be waiting for us at the border of Guinea and Liberia and that was still hours away.

I said to Paul, "Why don't you walk that way, and I'll walk this way," pointing to my right, "and perhaps we'll find someone." I had already looked under the hood of the Jeep I had been driving, and didn't see anything familiar that needed taking apart! I knew that if we did meet someone, we might not be able to speak his language. Paul spoke French, Maninka, and Kissi, but we were in Toma country and neither of us knew a word of that language.

As I walked down the road, I spied an old man working in his field and yelled to him in Kissi: "N se, A tyo kende, wa?" He simply lifted his hands in a gesture that let me know he didn't understand. I thought I would try French, though I knew the old codger would likely not understand that either. "Bonjour, Monsier," I yelled. "Comment allez-vous?" He replied in perfect French, "Tres bien, merci. Puis-je vous aider?" ("Fine, thank you. Can I help you?"). I could not believe it!

He had on an old Army coat, muddy as could be. He put down his hoe and began walking my way across the field. I was beginning to wonder what I would say to him. I was certain he didn't know anything about vehicles (and there weren't that many running around these parts!) but appreciated the fact that he appeared friendly, at least from a distance!

When he arrived by my side on the road, I explained to him what had happened and that I didn't know what to do next. I asked him how far away the next village was. He told me it was about a 15 minute walk "over there"---and he pointed to a grove of trees on a large hill some distance away.

"Can I see inside your vehicle?" he queried. "Yes," I said, but wondered why he asked. When we arrived at the Jeep, he opened the door and slid in. "Let me have the keys," he said confidently. I knew the car couldn't go anywhere because the gears didn't function so I gave him the keys.

He started the vehicle, put his foot on the clutch, tried the gearshift, and then said with some authority, "Looks to me like it may be your clutch disc." I was startled! In reality, I was speechless. Here was an African, a man of the bush, with us was in the middle of nowhere, and he is telling *me* what is wrong with my vehicle. All he had done was put his foot on the clutch and moved the gearshift!

Could he possibly know? It wasn't long before I found out. This old Toma man had been in the French Army and had served in Vietnam as a mechanic. More specifically, he was a clutch mechanic and had worked on Jeeps over there. God had placed him right in this village, right in this field, at this exact time, just for me. At least that's the only way I could interpret what was going on. A coincidence? I don't think so.

Could you believe it? I had always traveled with my tools but, on this occasion, being in a hurry to leave for this trip, I had left them in the garage at home. The man told me he had some tools and trotted off to his village to procure them. When he returned, he had three items in his hand: an old, broken (?) adjustable wrench, a pair of pliers, and an ancient screwdriver.

"You can't do much with those," I told him. But he did. He knew exactly what to do. While he did mangle the heads of some bolts, before long he had taken off the housing that held the clutch plate which he found broken in five pieces. I was happy and devastated at the same time. There were no Jeep parts in Guinea that I knew of, and certainly not where we were.

The old man told me I could wait by the road, hoping another vehicle would come by to take me to N'Zerekore and then go from there to Liberia. Certainly there would be Jeep parts somewhere in the capital, Monrovia. But how would I get there without a visa? How many days would it take? How? Who? What? I was just full of questions.

Suddenly the man began to trot towards his village again. "Wait, here Mister," he said. Where could I go? And off he ran. It was less than an hour later that he returned with a wooden box in his hand. In that crusty old box were two items that this old soldier had brought back from Vietnam: an old brake band, and a clutch disc that just fit my Jeep!

The old gentleman knew just what to do. He siphoned some gasoline from the Jeep to wash off the grease and dirt on the clutch disc. Then he went to the edge of the forest and cut off some palm branches that had rough, needle-like edges which he used to "sandpaper" the disc. When he had finished preparing it for installation, he put it in its proper place, tightened up the housing and within three hours I was on my way.

Wow! God had cared for little ol' me. Here I was, in just my second term as His servant overseas, and He was showing me His love, His wisdom, His grace, His miraculous care for one of His own. I had known of the miracles in my father's life as he shared with his children some of his past experiences. Why wouldn't God just keep acting like God and continue to show His love to the next generation?

I told that old Toma man that we were children of God and that his being there to help us was no accident. Paul and I even prayed with him, thanking him profusely for all that he had done for us. He would accept no payment from us. Now I wonder if he was an angel in disguise.

We arrived at the Liberian border just as the Millers pulled in. They had brought with them some large white chickens from the States. Doug agreed to sell me a large white rooster which

I took back with me to present to the old man who had helped us with the Jeep. He accepted it graciously. We also gave him, once again, the message of the gospel which includes more blessings than one could ever dream of. The Savior cares for His children. I will never need additional proof of that truth.

Chapter 10
Two Beautiful Blessings

We had been married more than ten years and had no children. God knew we wanted some! We had prayed, consulted different specialists, medical and otherwise, and we had asked the Lord to open the door for adoption if that was His will for us.

At the time, my father was District Superintendent of the Southwestern District of the C&MA but Dr. Richard LeTourneau asked if he would agree to be the Executive Vice-President of Letourneau College. Richard LeTourneau's father was ill and he had no choice but to assume the leadership of the LeTourneau Corporation. He could hardly fulfill that position and take leadership of the college as well.

When my father, Richard Harvey, agreed to take that position, he and my mother moved to Longview, Texas to help lead the college. At the same time he continued as District Superintendent of the Southwestern District. Peggy and I were on furlough (home assignment) at this time, and were able to move into the lovely district parsonage, which my folks had just vacated in Dallas.

While there we heard about an adoption agency in Oklahoma City, Oklahoma. We talked to the personnel there, filled out the necessary forms and waited. It wasn't long until we heard that a baby might be available for us. When we went to talk to them about this possible happy circumstance, it turned out they offered us *two* babies, born three days apart.

Talk about excitement! There were so many questions to be answered. Could we afford the expense of adopting two babies at once? Would the State of Oklahoma even permit it? If they did, would the state in which we lived approve? After all, we were living in Texas, the adoption was to take place in Oklahoma, and we were planning to move to Nebraska before crossing the ocean again to Guinea, West Africa. Roadblocks seemed almost insurmountable, though to us it appeared that God had opened wide the door and we wanted to walk through it!

The adoption agency in Oklahoma said it was fine with them if we adopted both babies; they only wanted to see if the home we were living in was suitable. When someone from the agency came to Dallas to see the home we were habitating at the time, they were impressed. The district parsonage was more than adequate! "Come pick up the babies!" we heard over the phone on that cold January day. We were on our way.

The babies were three weeks old when they were given over to us. What a day that was! We left the agency with two precious gifts in our arms and headed towards Dallas, stopping, I remember, at a Dairy Queen to celebrate—and change diapers! One of the babies, the oldest, was a beautiful baby girl. We named her Judith Dawn. The other blessing, just three days younger, was a handsome baby boy. We named him James David. How rich we had become in a matter of hours! God was so good to us!

We knew, however, that this was just the beginning in more ways than one. The babies were not officially ours as yet, as we had to appear in court in Dallas in a few weeks. The judge was to determine if we were suitable parents, if the circumstances surrounding the adoptions were conducive to this being proper procedure, and if we were financially capable of supporting the "twins."

In the meantime, Texas representatives from their social services department came to inspect the home, talk to us, ask many questions and then report back to the authorities. We waited anxiously for the date to be set when we would appear before the court so we could be told the final verdict. We could not even bear to think of anything but a decision in our favor. In a short time the babies had already become an integral part of our lives. We loved them so!

When the phone rang to let us know the court date was set, our praying for wisdom accelerated. On the morning of the court appointment we dressed in our finest to appear before the judge. I will never forget that day! I was one nervous father-in-waiting. Peggy appeared to be more calm than I as we drove over to the courthouse.

We sat in a room with other people who were there for other reasons, I am sure. When our names were called, we got up and walked slowly into the room where the judge was seated behind a large, dark wood judicial bench. In his hands he held what looked like a sheaf of manila folders.

"David and Margaret Harvey," he began. "You appear to be seeking to take on a very large responsibility at this time. As I have looked over these papers concerning your desire to adopt, it appears that nothing is usual about this case. You are desiring to adopt two babies, not one; you are living in Texas, have received these children from Oklahoma, and I note that you are moving soon to Omaha, Nebraska."

My hands were sweating and I felt that we were on a slippery slope. The judge continued: "What is more, I see that later this year you plan to return to West Africa. Is all of this correct? Is there a hospital close to where you will be serving in Africa?"

"Yes, your honor," I replied, trying to sound like it was all normal to me. "There is a hospital about 25 miles from where we live." I did not dare explain to him what *kind* of hospital it was. He may have known something about hospitals in Africa. I thought that he may have even done some research on that. "My wife is a registered nurse too" I quickly added.

"This is all so unusual," the judge went on. "Two babies, three states involved, living in Africa—and we have no way of knowing what your living conditions are there. I can see no real reason why I should grant you the approval for this adoption. I feel, however, that this is the right thing to do. I too believe in God and believe that He will guide you in raising the children. I approve the adoption!"

I was faint and beyond feeling. I was more than overjoyed. "Thank you, your honor," I replied and reached up to accept the papers he held out in his hand. We were now the parents of the two most beautiful babies in the world! God had once again manifested his love, mercy, and grace to us. Peggy and I left the courtroom in a hurry and when we reached the car, we held hands and offered a prayer of thanksgiving to our God for the gifts we would be allowed to keep as our own. We knew it would not be long until we would present them back to Him.

Over forty years have passed since those traumatic events. Judy and her husband, JP, are now serving as missionary houseparents in Dakar, Senegal. Jim lives in Denver with his lovely wife, Emily, and works as an energy consultant. God has shown His faithfulness to us all and He alone is to be praised.

Chapter 11
"Please Forgive Me"

When we arrived in Guinea for our third term, we felt we had returned to a different place than where we had left. At least it seemed that way to us. While we were on home assignment, President Sekou Toure of Guinea had issued an edict that all missionaries had to leave the country. God intervened and the president allowed a few missionaries to remain. We were among the few allowed to return!

The only missionaries permitted to remain were those at the Telekoro Bible Institute, a few at the Mamou children's school, and the director and his wife in the capital city of Conakry. Among those not permitted to return were my wife's parents, Michael and Helen Kurlak, who had been in Guinea since the 1920s. For the next 20 years, the maximum number of missionaries in the country hovered between twelve and fifteen.

The year was 1967 and we were permitted to return to the Bible school which was now being taught in the French language. Prior to this time, the courses had been taught in the Maninka language which was the trade language of the country. We were becoming somewhat proficient in French so we were permitted to return and begin teaching there. My wife also did quite a bit of dispensary work as well as helping with the births of a number of babies.

Meanwhile, our own family had doubled! On one occasion we made a trip to the Wesleyan Methodist hospital in Kamekwi, Sierra Leone. There we were able to obtain some vaccinations for our children and have them checked over by a very friendly American doctor. We also planned to go to Freetown to stock up on some food items. It was no easy task to arrive at this hospital, however.

While traveling through a small village in Sierra Leone in our pickup truck, a pregnant sheep darted across in front of the truck. Thud! It was so sudden that I had killed the sheep before I hardly had time to brake. People from the village appeared to be running all over the place, especially making a beeline towards our truck!

As I rolled down my window, three large men were suddenly at the vehicle. One dropped down in front of the front tires, one was lying down behind the rear tires, and two large black arms were through my window with his hands firmly gripping the steering wheel. It was obvious that I was not going anywhere!

"Please forgive me," I said. I was already reaching for my wallet to offer them "salt money." This is the custom there. If someone kills an animal by accident, one gives them a little money to help with what is needed in the preparation of the meal that would be forthcoming from the killed calf, goat, sheep, dog or whatever. Because this involved a pregnant sheep, however, they were in no mood for just "salt money."

There was really little money in my possession at the time. I might have had about $25.00 and that was in Guinea currency. Our plan was to cash a check in Sierra Leone to obtain that currency in order to purchase some supplies in Freetown.

The men who were yelling at us were very unhappy. I told them our predicament but I am sure they did not believe me. Besides that, it was obvious they were going to try and take advantage of the situation since we were evident strangers to that neck of the woods. They yelled and cajoled, threatened and did everything possible to frighten us. And they succeeded!

Peggy was leaning against her door crying. Our two babies were between us in car seats and as we spoke to the men about the need to get on our way due to the heat, the babies' health and other matters, the men began to calm down little by little. After a period of about thirty minutes, they agreed that the sum of about ten dollars would be sufficient. The man holding the steering wheel let loose of his grip and I started to breathe normally again.

That man ordered the other two who were on either end of the vehicle to get off the ground and then told us to go. We went without much hesitation! About a mile down the road we stopped, paused to give thanks to the Lord for protection and allowing us to be free to travel again. Life in a foreign land has its difficulties. God is indeed "a very present help in time of trouble."

Chapter 12
A True Snake Story

Almost all West African missionaries have their snake stories, or so I am told. And I am sure that all of them are true. Would a missionary ever tell a story that wasn't? I know all about this story as my wife and I were together when it happened and she can verify every detail of this fascinating adventure! We all know about the big fish that got away. This is about a big snake that didn't.

We had left the town of Kissidougou where I had been meeting with a number of Kissi pastors regarding church business. Darkness was beginning to fall as we made our way back to our home in Yende. We were about ten kilometers from our village when we spied a long log lying on the road. At least it *looked* like a log.

"That's not a log, that's a snake!" my wife yelled as the lights of the vehicle more clearly illuminated the lengthy creature. There, moving ever so slowly across the dirt road was a python which looked enormous to us. It turned out to be 15 feet, four inches long. It had a small sheep in its belly (we discovered later).

We could not see the python's head. It had already entered the tall elephant grass and was moving at a snail's pace even as we stopped the car some ten feet from its squirming body. I took out my .22 rifle, put in a shell, rested it on the window ledge, and aimed at where I imagined the head might be. Two shots rang out, but the snake slithered on like it didn't hear a thing!

As we descended from the vehicle, one of us (I can't remember which one), recalled that someone had said something about catching a python by the tail. They had said that if you step on its tail, it would raise it up and you could then put a rope's loop around it, tighten it, and pull the snake out! We decided to try it.

I had a rope in the car so we fashioned a loop, then I stepped on the tail of the snake. Peggy had the loop ready to put on its tail when it raised it up. I had my gun all cocked and ready to shoot should the snake decide to turn our way. Unbelievably, the python did just what we had been told. It raised its tail and quickly my wife placed the loop over its tail and we pulled it tight. The snake was trying to go one way and we were pulling as hard as we could to get the whole thing onto the road.

We were getting nowhere. Down the road we saw a strong, young man walking our way and I yelled, "*Hun nanun, ma mara na*" ("Come here and help us"). He asked me, "What are you doing?" I replied: "I have a big snake here and we need help to pull it out of the grass." "Good-bye" he answered, and started to turn around in the other direction.

"No, please come and help us," I shot back. "I'll give you fifty cents." He probably thought we were insane, but he came and got on the far end of the rope and started to help pull. We were so excited at this point that I forgot the obvious. All I had to do was tie the end of the rope to the vehicle and back up and we would have easily pulled the snake from the grass. But I was hardly thinking clearly at this point.

Inch by inch the snake was now being pulled back to the center of the road and, within minutes, there it was, all 15 feet of him (or her) curled up now in a circle on the road. The python's head was now resting on its body and my gun was now poised just about a foot away from its head. I am a pretty good shot at 12 inches!

Bang! Bang! I shot it twice to make sure it was really dead. This would make several good meals for our yardman and his family, after I had it skinned, of course. But first we had to get it into the truck and that took all the strength we had. Perhaps because it was night, perhaps because the snake was so large, or perhaps because we were just amateurs at this kind of thing, it seemed like all our strength just drained from us and we barely got the python in the truck.

I gave the man one dollar for his help and he was very grateful. I don't remember witnessing to him at this point. Even missionaries miss opportunities at times. But I did thank the Lord for His protection and we were soon on our way again towards our village.

It was late at night by now and when we arrived home I put the snake in a 55 gallon drum (how I got it in there I do not remember). The next morning I went to my missionary colleague's house to tell him of this fabulous tale. He would certainly be impressed.

"I got one bigger than that" he replied when I told him my tale. "That unsympathetic old so-and-so," I thought as he rambled on about the python he had killed a couple of nights earlier when he was out on an evangelistic trip with the local pastor.

He told me of how he had come upon a python about to eat a calf it had squeezed to death and how, with his 12-guage shotgun he had blown its head off. Then he told me how the snake had wrapped itself around the calf and crushed it. I sat there amazed at his even more astounding tale.

It then hit me like a lightning bolt. This is a picture of the situation in which we were living. Satan, the big Snake, had wrapped himself around these people and was squeezing them to death, so to speak. They needed to be set free! Only the truth of the gospel could do it. We had that truth. We had better use every opportunity that God gave us to declare it to people who had no other way to hear the message.

The skin of the python we killed is now in my office closet. It is still there after almost 50 years of being shown to people in many churches and schools around the country. It still reminds me of what that big Serpent continues to do on the continent of Africa. Only the Son of Man can set people free. And when He does, they are free indeed!

Chapter 13

Lassa Fever

The year was 1969 and, in the town of Lassa, Nigeria, two missionary nurses died suddenly of a then unknown virus. They were the first known of many –now in the thousands— to succumb to what is now referred to as Lassa fever. This fever is associated with occasional epidemics during which the case-fatality rate can reach 50 percent.

The countries in West Africa where this disease is recognized are Guinea, Liberia, Sierra Leone and Nigeria. It may have a geographical range beyond these countries but that is unknown at this time. The number of Lassa virus infections per year in West Africa is estimated at 100,000 to 300,000. Obviously, the estimates are difficult to verify as surveillance for cases of the disease is not uniformly performed.

When Mrs. Carrie Moore, a missionary to the Kissi tribe living at the Telekoro Bible Institute, became sick in August of 1965, no one knew immediately what she had. Mrs. Moore became very sick and eventually lost her hair and her hearing. Deafness is the most common complication of Lassa fever. It was discovered later that this is what Mrs. Moore contracted. Lassa Fever had been suffered in other West African countries *before* it was named in Nigeria in 1969.

Mrs. Moore was our Kissi language teacher. She supervised our learning of that language and was instrumental in the first translation of a good part of the Kissi New Testament and of many hymns. We were often with her and thoroughly enjoyed her enthusiasm for life and her love of the Kissi people. At the time of Mrs. Moore's illness, we didn't know how Lassa fever was transmitted.

We have found that it is not transmitted by casual contact. The host of the Lassa virus is a rodent known as the "multimammate rat." These rodents breed frequently and produce large numbers of offspring. They shed the virus in urine and droppings. The fact is that the virus can be transmitted through touching objects or eating food contaminated by these materials or through cuts and sores.

Donald Loose, another teacher at the Bible institute, became sick in 1967. The third person at the Bible school to contract the virus was Paul Ellenberger. That was in February, 1968. He came down with the disease a year and a half after Mrs. Moore but did not lose any hair and his hearing was unaffected. It was the sickest, however, that he had ever been! He is now (some 40 years since the disease was first discovered) 84 years old at this writing and quite healthy.

I was the fourth person on our station to contract Lassa fever. One of my blood samples was flown to the CDC in Atlanta, Georgia, to confirm that this was really the cause of my sickness in 1969. The blood test was positive for this disease.

What I remember is a low-grade fever lasting a long time: diarrhea, vomiting and the most uncomfortable feeling one can imagine. At first we thought it was malaria or the flu, which is usually the first thing one thinks of in Africa when sickness comes. I can still remember a thick blackness, a darkness that seemed to envelop the room in which I was lying. I remember crying out to God for deliverance in Jesus' name. This sickness was so prolonged, however, that my parents wrote to the field asking that I be sent home. I was not ready for that!

When one is sick and feverish, he often does not remember things that might have occurred at the time of the sickness. There is *one* thing, however, that I distinctly do remember. God gave me a very heightened appreciation of our Kissi brothers and sisters in Christ. On one occasion, almost the entire group of Kissi pastors came and knelt around my bed, pleading before the Lord to spare my life and bring me back into service again. God answered those prayers!

That was my worst sickness in the country of Guinea. I was to experience an even greater test while in Nigeria. But that is for later. Needless to say God was merciful to this child of His, and I will always be grateful for the care, love, and prayers of my wife, the missionary personnel on the station at Telekoro, and of our Kissi brothers who steadfastly held me up before the Lord.

Chapter 14
Only God Could Do It!

A message came from our International Ministries office in Colorado requesting that I pray about an opportunity to minister in southeastern Nigeria. A fairly large group of believers were interested in joining the Alliance and wanted to meet with a C&MA representative. They desired to hold evangelistic services in Port Harcourt, a large eastern Nigerian city, and requested that I be the evangelist for those meetings.

After obtaining what I felt was divine direction--and the proper documentation-- I flew from Conakry to Lagos and then boarded a flight for Port Harcourt. Since this was my first trip to Nigeria, I was hardly ready for all of the hullabaloo this would involve. When I descended from the plane in Lagos, I was mobbed by young men wanting to carry my suitcase, my briefcase, and it seemed as if they wanted to carry me!

Taxi drivers came storming to my side, trying to grab my belongings and usher me into their cab to take me to the national airport some distance away from the international airport where we had landed. When I arrived at the national airport I had a difficult time understanding the English announcements coming over the speakers.

When I saw scores of people rushing to a flight I just followed along. I would ask if that was the plane for Port Harcourt. When I finally found the right one, there was literally a mob of folk trying to squeeze up the stairs to get into the plane. No single line, mind you, just a crowd of eager, noisy folk shoving and pushing to get on the plane. It was almost as if I were lifted toward the stairs.

Later, I found out that more tickets are sold for each flight than there are seats on the plane and it was "first come, first seated." I remember on one of these flights (I was to take 15 of them) one passenger's coat was caught in the door of the plane as it was closed. The passenger was hanging on outside as the plane began to roll down the runway. People were screaming at the top of their voices and finally the plane stopped and he was unceremoniously let loose on the runway!

When our plane arrived in Port Harcourt about an hour later than scheduled, I was met by Reverend Onakalah, the leader of this group of believers who had chosen the name of The Savior's Evangelical Church. When they eventually joined the C&MA it was quite a long name to paint on their banners and over some of their churches: *The Savior's Evangelical Church of the Christian and Missionary Alliance.*

The first evangelistic service was already in progress when we arrived at the large soccer field in Port Harcourt. The organizers of this event had parked two large flatbed trucks back to back. This became a rather large stage where the praise band and the dignitaries were to be placed.

As I looked over the soccer field, I saw that there were already hundreds of folk who had gathered and were watching a film being shown on a large screen. I learned that their typical evangelistic service was comprised of lively singing, a Christian film shown, and then the speaker would be presented. The speaker, however, was usually presented at some interesting point in the film. At a very crucial moment in the film's story, the projector would be turned off and the announcement would be made: "And now here is the evangelist of the evening." The audience would then listen to the speaker hoping he wouldn't be too long as they wanted to see the end of the film!

This was my introduction to what would be a series of evangelistic meetings over the next few months and years. The series of meetings would usually last for eight days, from Sunday to Sunday and on that final day a trained worker would be left to guide into deeper biblical truth those who had responded to the messages.

I was impressed. These people sang with gusto, prayed fervently, appeared to be dedicated to Lord and wanted others to know who Jesus is. The response was overwhelming. During that first week in Nigeria, well over 200 people responded to give their hearts to the Master! I was just beginning to learn why so many Ibo people were ready to give their lives over to Jesus Christ. It certainly wasn't my preaching. I'll tell you the secret in the next chapter.

Chapter 15

The Secret

I had been asked by the leader of the Savior's Evangelical Church (SEC) if I wanted to join their daily prayer meetings for the evening evangelistic services. I was eager to join these dozen or so Nigerian believers as they appeared so eager to be involved in the Lord's work. I had been quite impressed by the vitality of the evangelistic team of which I had been a part in Port Harcourt.

The group decided to meet on the second story of a bombed-out building near the heart of the city. The destruction to this building, and so many others in the area, had been the result of the Nigerian Civil War, also known as the Nigerian-Biafran War which took place from 1967-1970.

On the second floor of this partially destroyed structure there were about 15 chairs arranged in a circle. They were all filled when I arrived at about nine in the morning. Immediately, one of the men stood up and offered me his chair. I felt it wasn't proper to take his chair, though I knew that as a stranger, and the invited guest, it would be improper to refuse. I sat down and immediately this group of believers began to sing.

It was almost angelic to my ears. With softness yet strength, their voices in harmony, they began to sing choruses in Ibo and in English. I joined in and knew that this praise to the King was rising up as a sweet odor to our Lord. Some Scripture was read, and then a few remarks were made in the Ibo language which was quite foreign to my ears.

Then the leader said softly, "Let us kneel before our great God and intercede for the people of Port Harcourt. Let us ask the Creator to move among the people here so that many more might recognize His love shown in Jesus Christ. He answered our prayers last evening and we want to see even more to bow before Him in repentance."

As one man, it seemed, each person dropped quickly to his knees and I joined them, kneeling on broken cement and stone. The damage to this upstairs room had left the floor totally mangled so that stones and pieces of cement covered the entire floor. Everything was uneven at the place I was kneeling and the stones and broken cement seemed to bite sharply into my knees.

I was trying to concentrate on praying but I found it very difficult to kneel on such a rough surface. I looked around at the others kneeling before the Lord and it did not appear that anyone else was having the same problem as I. They were all agreeing with the one praying and I was left to fidget on my knees while trying to concentrate on seeking the Lord. Did they all have "camel knees" as the Apostle James was reputed to have had?

More than once I shifted to a one-knee kneeling position. Then I would sort of squat down trying to save my knees from the piercing stones which left me so uncomfortable. Once again I would return to a kneeling position. I tried to do this quietly but it was obvious that my movement had been somehow noticed by at least one of the others praying beside me.

In one of the most embarrassing moments of my life, I suddenly felt someone gently bump me. One of the men had found a piece of cardboard and was trying to slide it under my knees! Oh what discomfort. But this time, it was not from the stones or cement pieces digging into my knees. Rather, it was from the shameful embarrassment I felt at being such a wimp when praying on my knees.

I was the evangelist. I was the one who had come to help theses people in their spiritual service to the Lord. I was the one who was to model what it meant to be a true follower of the Lord. Yet I was the one struggling to stay on my knees for such a long time.

An hour passed. Then two hours went by until 11:30 had been reached. "Let us stand and sing," the leader said and I perhaps was the first one on my feet! No one was happier than I to stand and sing. When the meeting was over, the leader told the group they would meet again in the afternoon, from 3:00 to 5:00, to continue their prayer for the evening service.

The secret was out. The reason for the large number of people responding to the invitations given each evening was obvious. It had nothing to do with the speaker, nor the program, whether it was the excellent praise band or the exciting film they would show. It was prayer: fervent, non-hurried, intense, believing prayer.

That was not the last time I would take part in such a glorious event. Three months later I was back in Nigeria and invited to pray for an apparently demonized lady. The prayers were to start at midnight. As I left the house in which I was staying at the edge of the forest, I could see lantern after lantern piercing the darkness in the forest, as people came down the forest paths to intercede on behalf of this needy one.

What a precious sight. I'll never forget it as long as I live. The forest was filled with little spots of light here and there as believers gathered to seek deliverance for one of their friends. I was the missionary there to help them. I was the one invited to teach them how to know God in a more intimate way. I knew immediately, however, that I was witnessing something that the Lord wanted *me* to learn about the importance of prayer at all hours of the day and night. And God was to work even more wondrously in the days ahead.

Chapter 16
A Demonstration of God's Grace

It was the closing night of my first week in Port Harcourt and the subject I had chosen for that last evangelistic service was that of "pardon." I wanted to let the listeners know that God would pardon them completely for any sin if they trusted the sacrifice which He offered in His Son.

The crowd appeared to be listening intently and when the invitation was given there were probably over 50 people who responded. This created a happy problem (not enough workers to help the many who came), as the leaders of the SEC and I descended from the beds of the flatbed trucks to come down and deal with those kneeling on the grass of the field.

During the week I noticed a middle-aged woman sitting on a three-legged stool listening intently to the messages. Now, on this closing night, she had come forward. As I reached the edge of the grass where she was kneeling, she reached out and grabbed hold of my shoes. She spoke to me in Ibo and I, of course, did not understand her words.

I called over to Reverend Onakalah, the leader of the SEC, to come and help me when he was finished with the one with whom he was dealing. When I tried to back away from the lady who was holding on to my shoes, she just held on tighter than ever. I waited, somewhat patiently, until brother Onakalah came to my aid.

"She has been trying to talk to me," I told brother Onakalah, "but I haven't been able to understand her. She doesn't appear to speak any English. Could you please help me?" Reverend Onakalah reached down and took the lady's hands from my shoes and simply said, "Tell me what you want to ask him."

When she replied, he then turned to me and said, "She wants to know if what you said is all true." "Of course it's true;" I said, "it came from God's book." She then began to weep and grabbed hold of my shoes again. This went on for some time. It was an uncomfortable feeling and I finally said to Reverend Onakalah, "Please tell her to release her hands from my shoes and believe that what God said is true. He will forgive every sin if we ask Him to forgive us and if we want to forsake our sin to follow Him."

This lady, whom I will call Kumba, then said: "You do not know what I have done. If you knew what I had done, you would know how angry God would be with me." When I replied that God loved her and wanted to forgive her, she finally told us that she was a prostitute. She then went on to tell us that she was more than that!

She began to tell us that her husband had come home the week before and surprised her, finding her in bed with another man. As he tried to fight with her and the strange man, Kumba picked up an iron that was on a table and hit her husband repeatedly on the head with it until he fell and died. She buried him in their backyard. She cried out, "I am not only a prostitute but also a murderer. Could God forgive me?"

"Yes, He will, if you ask Him," I said. Reverend Onakalah then told her again the Calvary story and she said she believed. Brother Onakalah then took her hand and placed it in mine and said to me: "Brother Harvey, take her hand and welcome her into the Kingdom of God!" I did and Kumba began to cry tears of joy and thanked the Lord for saving her. It was an hour of transformation. The whole expression on Kumba's face changed radically when she realized that God had actually forgiven her.

I believe I was as happy as she. I had never seen such a transformed face as I saw that evening. God had radically changed her, brought her into the family of God and made her a new creature in Him.

The next day the pastor and her friends accompanied Kumba to the police station where she confessed what she had done and what she had become. She was incarcerated there in Port Harcourt and I never saw her again as I had to return to Guinea. I will see her again, however, in the mansions above. Amazing grace is still in operation in our day.

Chapter 17
A Choice to Make

We had only been in Nigeria a couple of months. Peggy and I had agreed to settle there and work among the Christians of the Savior's Evangelical Church in a teaching and evangelizing ministry. We were housed in a rather nice dwelling owned by members of the church who were good friends of the Onakalahs. The name of the small town was Umuderim.

I came down with a fever which I thought would pass with time. My temperature kept rising and my wife, Peggy, did everything a skilled nurse could do. We had no vehicle at the time, but could be chauffeured by Reverend Onakalah to any pharmacy in the area. Peggy was able to procure what antimalarial drugs she thought suitable. The fever kept raging, however.

I fell into a coma. As there were no telephones or email possibilities at that time, my wife simply prayed and asked God for wisdom in how to care for the situation at hand. We were in the middle of nowhere as far as we were concerned and there didn't seem any way out of this seeming disaster.

Down in Congo and Gabon, Rev. David Kennedy was finishing a trip to that area of the world and was on his way back to the States. God, in His mercy, brought us to David's mind and he thought "Perhaps I'll stop off in Nigeria and pay the Harveys a visit." At the time He had no clue that God had placed us on his heart during a critical time in our lives.

When David arrived in Umuderim he was shocked to find that I was just coming out of a coma and still very sick. "We will have to evacuate you folks out of here," was David's comment when he saw my weakened condition. "Do you want to fly back to the States or remain in Africa?" was his question to us. This was a big choice for us. We didn't want to give up our African ministry so for us the answer came quickly. "If we can find a place in Africa, we would just as soon stay and recuperate on our adopted continent."

Mr. Kennedy made the decision to evacuate us to the Baptist hospital in Ferekessedougou in the Ivory Coast. There the doctors found that I had cerebral malaria and treated me with a large dose of quinine and other anti-malarial drugs. Slowly I began to return to normal health and was sent to Bouake to recuperate.

Another choice needed to be made. I could either return to Guinea to teach at the Bible Institute there or remain in the Ivory Coast for the next two years. The national church leaders in the Ivory Coast had asked that Theological Education by Extension (TEE) be begun there and I had taken some courses in that area while obtaining my Master's Degree.

I agreed to stay and work with the mission and church in the Ivory Coast. It was the beginning of a new ministry for us which was blessed by God and used for the extension of His Kingdom there. We were accepted with open arms by the missionary personnel in Bouake and began to teach in that city and eventually in many other towns and villages in the Ivory Coast.

The work was not without its challenges, however, as the church leadership wanted first to be instructed themselves so as not to know less than the average church member! Our goal, however, was to train lay leaders in the many churches there to know God's Word more fully and then to be able to teach others. While waiting for the church leadership to give their final okay to the project, I began teaching a number of courses at the Bible school in Yamousoukro.

Within a few weeks we were able to begin the process of teaching lay leaders in the Bouake area and eventually began traveling to cities and towns from Soubre to San Pedro and from Gagnoa to Abidjan. What a joy to see men study the Word and then *continue on* for weeks and months in the future. It took cerebral malaria to move me from Nigeria to the Ivory Coast, but, as always, God's plans for us are always the best for His children and the extension of His Kingdom.

Chapter 18

Mixed Emotions

Taking or sending your children to an MK school has been a rather traumatic experience for most parents, and we were no exception. By the time our children had reached the age for entering first grade, there was no MK school in Guinea and our only option was to take them to Sierra Leone. In that country, the Missionary Church Association (MCA) was directing a school for missionary children in Kabala.

The trip over the border in the rainy season was enough to challenge anyone's emotional stability. Then one faced the necessity of leaving your children standing on the dorm steps while you pulled away in the van. Since we only had two children, and both were the same age, the wrenching experience of leaving them for the first time is indelibly impressed on my mind.

I don't like to go there in my memory, preferring to close the door on those experiences and live life in the present. Recalling those moments for this writing is not a pleasant event. The trips over the border bring a kind of trauma to my memory that only those who have traveled those roads could comprehend.

When our children began attending school in Sierra Leone, the borders were officially closed due to the nature of the Guinea government at that time. Special papers or visas were necessary for crossing into Sierra Leone. There were check points along the way and an always-questioning border patrol with which one would have to negotiate. The roads in the rainy season were indescribable.

It was always best to travel with other families. We usually had the privilege of traveling with the Andy Gardners or the Paul Ellenbergers, usually in the same van. That would make it at least bearable. There were rivers to go through or unbelievable bridges (we called them "non-bridges") to cross. We didn't always cross them by bridge. One time we were pulled through the river by a tractor. But that's another story.

I recall mixed emotions, emotions tied up with trying to reach our destination without losing our sanctification, and of the even deeper emotions of what lay ahead when the kids would be separated from mom and dad. I think of the range of events and emotions that stirred our minds and hearts: the gnawing dread of the "non-bridges" just ahead; the joyous laughing and singing of the kids in the rear of the van; the uncertain questioning of the custom agents, police and gendarmes at the border; the joy of renewing friendships with missionary colleagues in Sierra Leone; and the dreaded anticipation of leaving the kids standing on the dormitory porch as we returned home.

For the gospel's sake, all of these emotions appeared necessary. For the sake of extending God's Kingdom in Guinea, any sacrifice or experience could not be too great. Did not Abraham face the most grueling test of all? Can we even begin to compare what we were facing with what he faced for his love and obedience to the will of the Father?

It is all in the past right now. My own daughter and her husband are now facing separation from their children as they minister in Senegal and their three daughters are in college in the States. Yet there is still another emotion. That of deep joy in knowing that serving the Lord brings Him glory as we submit to His will and do His bidding as we understand it. Nothing can surpass that peace of heart when one knows he is pleasing the One who gave His own Son. Think of the emotions of that Son and Father.

When times of separation and hardship loom ahead in our life experiences, songs of inspiration or consecration seem more than just melodies on a song sheet. I am thinking now of one you may know: "It Will Be Worth It All When We See Jesus." Nothing is more true to this writer.

Chapter 19
An Unforgettable Bush Trip

I couldn't believe what was happening! It was 11:00 at night and I was in the middle of nowhere. It was difficult lifting up a prayer of thanksgiving for what we had just experienced. Let me tell you about it.

Almost every month I would make trips into either the Kissidougou or Guekedou districts where our Kissi tribe of about 160,000 people made their homes. On these trips I would usually travel with one of our Kissi pastors. Our distinct objective was to encourage the Kissi workers in these area churches and evangelize villages where little witness had gone on before.

On this particular trip we were in an area some distance from the large town of Kissidougou. I had already set up my aluminum cot and fixed the mosquito net so that I was prepared to sleep when the evening service was over. Before I left the hut however, to attend the meeting, a knock came at the door.

It was the Kissi pastor who had accompanied me on this trip. He was telling me that we had some opposition to our being in the village this evening, so if there was noise or some kind of commotion, he would try and handle it. He asked to pray together and then we left our hut to attend the service.

When we sang, gave testimonies and preached a simple gospel message, I was pleasantly surprised at the large number of Kissi men and women who said they wanted to follow the One who had paid such a price for their sin. We took quite a bit of time that evening to pray for the many who seemed genuinely interested in the message of love we had preached.

As I was finishing up admonishing one young man who had come to pray, the pastor came to me and said we would have to be moving on. It would be best if I returned to the hut, took down the mosquito net, folded up the aluminum cot, and left. We would be safer if we stayed in another village down the road. I told him that I would be ready in about 15 minutes.

When I got my belongings to carry them to the pick-up truck, I noticed the truck had a flat tire. "I must have run over some sharp piece of wood coming into the village," I thought. I set down a lantern some distance from the tire and began to jack up the truck. When I took off the tire and did a brief examination of it, I found that there was a nail in the tire.

After I put on the spare, we got into the truck and began traveling to the next village where the pastor had told me it would be best to spend the night. We had gone about a mile when I noticed the truck was not steering properly. There was a pull to the right. When I descended from the truck, flashlight in hand, I found that I had a flat front tire. Then I noticed that two other tires were low. When I examined them carefully, I found that nails had been pounded into each of the tires. I was not singing songs of praise at this time.

I tried to act victoriously in the midst of this circumstance but I found it difficult to be thankful for anything. I had already forgotten about the many who had responded just a couple of hours previous to the message of Christ's pardon for sin. And I remember asking the Lord to give me grace to get through this. I was one tired, dirty, frustrated, unhappy missionary.

Later I learned that the witchdoctor in the village we had been in hired some young men to pound nails in my truck's tires during our service. Now here we were, in the middle of nowhere, with midnight approaching, and I had three flat tires. When I checked the tire-patch kit which I always carried with me, I found that I had enough patches for two tires, perhaps, but certainly not for three. I didn't relish sleeping in the truck all night and then trying to get help in the morning. We had no other choice, however.

A motorcycle came by about six in the morning. The driver had some patches and glue with him in this out-of-the-way place and he sold them to me for a small sum. We were able to fix the last tire and get on our way. But I was unhappy. I had come all this way to preach the Word of Life and someone was pounding nails in my truck's tires.

God had to deal with me about that. Here, more than two dozen people had prayed to receive Jesus Christ as Savior, were now members of His Church, and I was complaining because I had to stay up one night fretting about some tire trouble.

Do you know what was even worse? The next month I received a letter from the pastor who had been with me on that trip asking that I return with him to that village for teaching. Guess what I told him. I actually sent him a message that was not entirely true. I told him I had other plans and asked if we could put it off for some time until I could fit it into my schedule!

Sure, I had some other plans. But I knew I could change them. Yet I was unwilling to do that because of the tire problem I so vividly remembered experiencing in that village. God had to work on me for at least a week until I finally wrote back a positive response to the pastor's request. I learned how carnal I was. But I also learned that there was forgiveness and that the grace of God is bigger than any problem—or perceived problem—that we might have. As I clearly remember, many blessings followed as new Christians were full of joy at learning new truths about the Savior and the holy walk He wants us to have with Him.

Chapter 20

Standing in the Plate

Speaking at a conference in the Guekedou Region was always an exhilarating experience for me. Just being there to hear the lively singing and the personal testimonies of transformed lives, and to fellowship with the believers of that area—this was just something of which I could not get enough.

At the annual Kissi conference held in Guekedou just before we were to head home on furlough, I was requested to speak on three occasions. On the closing Sunday evening we were all gathered under a large, palm leaf shelter built to hold about 500 delegates. It was crowded, the air was still, and it was unusually warm that evening. Yet, there was a spirit of anticipation that God was going to move among us.

Before I spoke, two converted witchdoctors wanted to tell how they had become friends after being enemies for so long. They told of their deliverance from Satan's clutches, and how they had met right there at that conference and desired to sing a song of praise to the Lord.

It was the most unusual song I had ever heard. They seemed to make it up as they went along. The music was not pleasant to my ears but the sounds of their redeemed voices lifted all of our spirits as God was praised for His transforming power that had operated in their lives. When it was time for me to speak, the audience had already been prepared by God's Spirit to hear His Word.

Just as I was about to go to the pulpit, however, the leader of the meeting got to his feet to announce that he had forgotten to take up the offering. While it seemed a bit unusual and out of place at that time, I had become accustomed to unusual and out-of-place events in African services!

The leader said: "I know that many of you who have come here do not have any extra funds to give and that is fine. God does not expect you to give what you do not have, but to give Him what you do possess. Give as unto the Lord."

The ushers with woven baskets began to go down the one large center aisle as well as outside the shelter. Seated on the platform, I was able to see that a young man was standing about a third of the way back on my left. He could not have been over fourteen years of age.

As the basket was passed down his "row," he took it in his hand, bent over and placed it on the floor. Then he just stepped into the basket with his head bowed. I watched as the lady next to him appeared to poke him, so he stepped out of the basket, bent down, picked it up and passed it along.

He was giving what he had. Where he had heard of such a thing, whether he had ever seen it done before . . . I have no idea. But I will never forget this act of giving and dedication. I suspect that God had nudged his heart and he had responded in the only way he knew how.

That act of giving made my service in Africa worth all that I had ever put into it. And what I had put into it was no doubt less than this young lad was giving. As the poet has written: "Only one life, t'will soon be passed; only what's done for Christ will last."

Chapter 21

Au revoir

Saying goodbye to Africa was not an easy thing. Saying *au revoir* (to the seeing again) made it a little easier. We have "seen again" that continent, having made three trips back to that land since we left West Africa in 1987.

God had permitted us to minister in three countries of West Africa: Guinea, Ivory Coast, and Nigeria. In each of these lands we worked with godly people, saw lost ones born into His Kingdom, and rejoiced as God thrust African laborers into His harvest fields.

When my ministry changed to working in a college setting with young people who believed God was calling them into ministry, I asked God to help me convey my love and concern for the lost of Africa to those whom I would be teaching. For the next twenty years it was my privilege to share what I had learned with those who were eager to be His overseas servants.

It was not an easy task. With deadlines, clocks on the walls, papers, tests, and a myriad of classes, students might not be able to "hear my heart." How can one be relaxed and stirred at the same time? How is it possible to convey one's passion when grades are what the students are thinking about, there are papers due, and there are so many other things which occupy one's mind in the classroom.

Yet four years can be a long time and some of the students would be rubbing shoulders with me for that long (hopefully not longer!). During those three or four years could I instill in them some lasting principles, concepts, but most of all *compassion*? That, I know, has to come from God, Himself.

The way we train people may not always include what God wants us to teach them! And it is certainly not the way Christ trained His disciples. Of course there is no way we can live and teach by example the way Christ did. But it can be somewhat frustrating trying to instill in the hearts of your students what you think is important to learn. There is no end to books, graphs, charts, overheads, whiteboards, films, lectures, facts, statistics, chapels, and talk. To help students *believe* that God is immutable, that He can transform lives, that knowing Him is what is essential, that trusting and loving Him is what life is all about, is that of which the end of education should consist. Developing a life of prayer, taking time for people, a life characterized by grace and meekness, this is what needs to be conveyed. It is no easy task.

In saying *au revoir* to Africa, I was not saying goodbye to ministry. I was only desiring to change my focus to influencing lives in the U.S. for the Kingdom of God. In my heart, I have never said goodbye to Africa. That is one reason I have written the stories in this small book. The dark continent has a way of stealing one's heart. May the God who has brought so many from darkness into light on that continent continue to inspire others to even greater exploits of love and service to the millions who have yet to hear.

Made in the USA
Charleston, SC
10 August 2011